WHEN STEAK WAS
A SHILLING A POUND

WHEN STEAK WAS A SHILLING A POUND

Written and illustrated by Margaret Chapman

PUBLISHED IN LONDON BY JUPITER BOOKS LIMITED MCMLXXVIII

First published in 1978 by
JUPITER BOOKS (LONDON) LIMITED
167 Hermitage Road, London N4 1LZ

Copyright © Margaret Chapman 1978

ISBN 0 906379 02 4

Composed in 14pt Linotronic Tiffany Light
by Optic Photosetting Limited, London,
and printed and bound in Spain.

When steak was a shilling a pound...
    and beef dripping was acceptable,
would any child turn up its nose
at the thought of chops again for dinner?

JOHANNIS
KING OF NATURAL TABLE WATERS
PROMOTES APPETITE
AIDS DIGESTION
AND PROLONGS LIFE
TO BE OBTAINED FROM CHEMISTS,
WINE MERCHANTS AND GOOD STORES
M. Chapman '75

INTRODUCTION

We live in the seventies . . . conventional products of the age . . . using, consuming, expecting and demanding. We groan if the car does not start . . . if we run out of sliced bread or soap-powder. We expect our beds to be heated, our food to be frozen or cooked, and our laundry to be done with the minimum of attention from ourselves. We demand light and warmth and entertainment at the flick of a switch. Our children accept these present-day benefits as of right . . . We as parents accept too, but vaguely recall a time before drip-dry shirts and polythene bags, when televisions were not compulsory, and pastry was rubbed from flour and lard at the kitchen table. But even we parents cannot remember when aeroplanes were not a feature in our lives, when cornflakes were unknown, when carpets were swept by hand and Monopoly was yet to be invented. How did they cope then, without telephones or cars . . . without aspirin or tins of beans or tooth-paste? What was it like with only a kitchen range for cooking, and every drop of hot water coming from a constantly simmering kettle on the hob? When hatters and glovers were everyday occupations . . . when Magic Lanterns were enthralling novelties . . . when contraception was in its infancy and most immunization still in the future . . . and electricity in the home was not ordinarily aspired to . . . What was it like? . . . How did they manage? . . . Are text-books, in dwelling on privations, too materialistic? . . . Are old ladies in recalling the past affectionately, looking back through rose-tinted glasses? . . .

We who were born too late, into a different generation, can only imagine . . .

WHEN STEAK WAS
A SHILLING A POUND

When steak was a shilling a pound . . .
   and beef dripping was acceptable,
would any child turn up its nose
   at the thought of chops again for dinner?

When tram-cars were still an innovation,
   too costly for everyday travel...
And women walked
      from Saturday shopping,
         loaded with parcels
            and children in tow,
         happily counting
            precious pennies saved...

. . . And men worked
        an eighty hour week,
    in heat of mills,
        and damp of mines,
    with laying-off at owner's whim,
        and no eventual pension . . .
. . . yet for twenty-two and six
still thought themselves lucky
                to have a job . . .

. . . And mothers rose at four or five
to fire boilers for the week's washing . . .
        scraping soap
            and boiling starch,
on slippery kitchen floors . . .
        and craving not for
            automatic dryers,
        but merely that it might not rain
                        that Monday . . .

M. Chapman

Who would not have envied the
'enterprising young lady' who,
due to a 'weak constitution',
could not do heavy work,
but who, imaginatively found
more than monetary reward in the occupation of,
setting off into the country
to dress the last season's hats
of the country ladies?

When God was seen as
a terrifying old man
beyond the clouds...
and children would walk
five miles to Sunday School...
and proudly receive
a Pilgrim's Progress
after a year's attendance.

When fêtes were fun,
and no-one needed
celebrities to help celebrate
on summer sports days...
and the 'World's Fattest Lady'
...or 'Thinnest Man',
were enough to fetch even parents
willingly
to carnivals...

M. Chapman.

... Before
canals and trees
were replaced
by
paddling pools and climbing
frames...

...And,
when education was a
recent privilege,
would not our children have gone
gratefully to school...
never scribbling in their
text-books
or complaining
that sums
were a waste of time?

M.Chapman.

Manchester was only
seven hours away from
London...
for those who could afford the
twelve-and-six
return...
...and no conservationist
had yet complained
about the dirt
of steam trains.

M. Chapman '75

Haworth was uncelebrated...
only too similar to
Bolton and Bradford
and Blackburn...
...resounding to the clash
of clogs on cobbles...
its claim
to Brontë fame,
yet to be exploited...

...Whilst
London's lurid attractions
were
still safely
hidden
in Whitechapel alleys...
and
Piccadilly Circus still
enjoyed
fashionable
respectability.

When the motor-car
    was an enthralling novelty,
        did anyone believe
            it could ever replace
the conventional
        cabs and carts...
    and even turn horses
        into luxuries?

M. Chapman.

When ice-creams were just
        ice-creams...
    and hot-dogs had yet to replace
    whelks and cockles
    on the stalls
        at Margate...

M. Chapman.

And,
    a stick and hoop
        or hopscotch
            was as much fun as
                a skateboard or bike...
    ...and educational toys
            were not even a gleam in a
                manufacturer's eye...

And,
when holidays were
one week in fifty-two,
how jubilant would be
those fortunate folks
on the Station Road,
those summer Saturdays...
with the cries of
'Carry your bags for tuppence',
ringing in their ears.

When the weighty gas-iron
                was new,
and women gladly gave away their flat-irons,
        and after years of ironing,
                by roaring fires
                        on hot summer's evenings,
        joined the rest of the world
                idling in the street's sunshine...

M. Chapman '74.

...When beer was
three ha'pence a pint,
   and men washed away the week's dirt
     in zinc baths
       before Saturday forays...
and children followed
with pre-Sabbath swills,
   in the same zinc bath,
    topped up from a simmering kettle,
     and who cared if the water
       was second or thirdhand...

And when
    ladies' winter knickers were
        one and threepence a pair new...
        but only
            sixpence secondhand...
and vast families
        of ten or twelve
            were not unusual...
    would any child object to
            hand-me-downs?

G. & R. ROSE'S
DEALERS IN CHILDREN'S WEAR SINCE 1876
END OF SEASON'S
GRAND SALE
ALL PRICES REDUCED BY AT LEAST 10%
CHILDREN'S CHEMISES 1/-
EDGE-TRIMMED 1/3
LACE INSERTION 1/11
COMBINATIONS from 2/1
FLANNELETTE NIGHTS 1/9
(CREAM from 1/9 PINK from 2/-)
KNICKERBOCKERS
PLAIN from 10½ LACE-EDGE
TRUNK-TYPE 1/-
all sizes
LOTS MORE GREAT REDUCTIONS
G. & R. ROSE
FOR SALE
VALUABLE
PLOT OF LAND
RESIDENTIAL AREA
HAWKSHAW AVE,
SUITABLE FOR
TWO SUPERIOR
DETACHED VILLAS
£600 each
M. Chapman

In days when pawn shops
    were full of frilly white dresses...
  in the week following
      the Wakes Walks...

...And high sport for boys
was tailing carts...
or dodging under the bellies
of moving horses...

...And
    when pocket-money was not
      a children's prerogative,
   what girls would not gladly
       earn
      a penny a week...
  toting breast-fed babies,
    to working mothers,
in their breakfast
      and lunch-breaks?

Diet was little considered...
But how ironic that
the woman who unwittingly
provided vitamins
by buying fresh fruit for her children,
was dismissed as
'indulgent and spendthrift'...

With station in life accepted...
    and the 'New Contraption'
    not even a working man's dream
        of the future...
    would anyone then feel the need
    to spy jealously
    on their neighbours'
        rich relations?

When doctors
        were not called in
            for cut knees
                and diarrhoea…
but
    advertizing was unrestricted,
    and wonder cures were claimed
            for any ailment…

Before
 telephones and ease of transport
  had strangely lead to
   a lessening of
    short communications,
 and a birth,
   death
     or shotgun marriage
      was sufficient for
      a week's good gossip...

And when
    babies were born
    at home
    with Grandmother directing
    and Great Aunts
    boiling kettles
    and comparing confinements...
did women really feel
        that they had let their husbands down
            if they produced girls?

M. Chapman '69.

When
   a decision to emigrate
      was almost irrevocable,
   and America's call for workers
      was answered by millions...
   who would foresee the crossing of
         the Atlantic
      cut to mere hours?

Before
    the divorce rate
        was one in four,
   and marriages were showers of rice
      and half the neighbourhood
        turning out to watch...

...And when a remarkable machine
could produce likenesses from only
    ten-second poses...
would anyone suspect that seventy
    years later, people might look at
        those faded sepia prints and wonder
            however did they cope in
                those different days?